BROADWAY SONGS FOR TWO

T0039525

Arrangements by Peter Deneff

ISBN 978-1-5400-1286-9

HAL•LEONARD®
7777 W. BLUEMOUND RD. P.O. BOX 13819 MILWAUKEE, WI 53213

Visit Hal Leonard Online at
www.halleonard.com

CONTENTS

ANY DREAM WILL DO

from JOSEPH AND THE AMAZING TECHNICOLOR® DREAMCOAT

TRUMPETS

Music by ANDREW LLOYD WEBBER
Lyrics by TIM RICE

BRING HIM HOME
from LES MISÉRABLES

TRUMPETS

Music by CLAUDE-MICHEL SCHÖNBERG
Lyrics by HERBERT KRETZMER
and ALAIN BOUBLIL

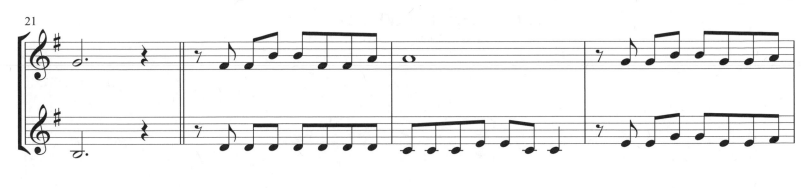

D.S. al Coda

CODA

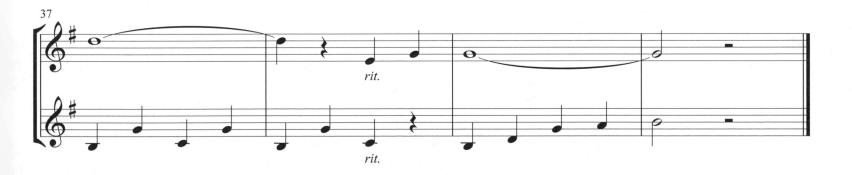

rit.

rit.

CABARET
from the Musical CABARET

TRUMPETS

Words by FRED EBB
Music by JOHN KANDER

EDELWEISS

from THE SOUND OF MUSIC

TRUMPETS

Lyrics by OSCAR HAMMERSTEIN II
Music by RICHARD RODGERS

FOR FOREVER
from DEAR EVAN HANSEN

TRUMPETS

Music and Lyrics by BENJ PASEK
and JUSTIN PAUL

HELLO, DOLLY!

from HELLO, DOLLY!

TRUMPETS

Music and Lyric by
JERRY HERMAN

I BELIEVE
from the Broadway Musical THE BOOK OF MORMON

TRUMPETS

Words and Music by TREY PARKER,
ROBERT LOPEZ and MATT STONE

I WHISTLE A HAPPY TUNE

from THE KING AND I

TRUMPETS

Lyrics by OSCAR HAMMERSTEIN II
Music by RICHARD RODGERS

IF I WERE A BELL

from GUYS AND DOLLS

TRUMPETS

By FRANK LOESSER

THE IMPOSSIBLE DREAM
(The Quest)
from MAN OF LA MANCHA

TRUMPETS

Lyric by JOE DARION
Music by MITCH LEIGH

MAMMA MIA

from MAMMA MIA!

TRUMPETS

Words and Music by BENNY ANDERSSON, BJÖRN ULVAEUS and STIG ANDERSON

MEMORY
from CATS

TRUMPETS

Music by ANDREW LLOYD WEBBER
Text by TREVOR NUNN after T.S. ELIOT

Slowly, with feeling

MY FAVORITE THINGS

from THE SOUND OF MUSIC

TRUMPETS

Lyrics by OSCAR HAMMERSTEIN II
Music by RICHARD RODGERS

ONE
from A CHORUS LINE

TRUMPETS

Music by MARVIN HAMLISCH
Lyric by EDWARD KLEBAN

POPULAR
from the Broadway Musical WICKED

TRUMPETS

Music and Lyrics by
STEPHEN SCHWARTZ

SEASONS OF LOVE

from RENT

TRUMPETS

Words and Music by
JONATHAN LARSON

SEVENTY SIX TROMBONES

from Meredith Willson's THE MUSIC MAN

TRUMPETS

By MEREDITH WILLSON

SUMMERTIME

from PORGY AND BESS®

TRUMPETS

Music and Lyrics by GEORGE GERSHWIN,
DuBOSE and DOROTHY HEYWARD
and IRA GERSHWIN

SUNRISE, SUNSET

from the Musical FIDDLER ON THE ROOF

TRUMPETS

Words by SHELDON HARNICK
Music by JERRY BOCK

TOMORROW
from the Musical Production ANNIE

TRUMPETS

Lyric by MARTIN CHARNIN
Music by CHARLES STROUSE

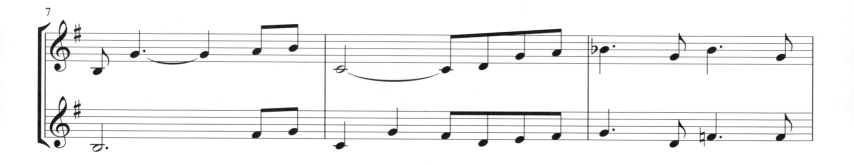

WHERE IS LOVE?

from the Broadway Musical OLIVER!

TRUMPETS

Words and Music by
LIONEL BART

YOU'VE GOT A FRIEND

featured in BEAUTIFUL: THE CAROLE KING MUSICAL

TRUMPETS

Words and Music by
CAROLE KING